His Princess

Prayers to My King

by Sheri Rose Shepherd

Multnomah Gifts

Multnomah Books

HIS PRINCESS: PRAYERS TO MY KING
© 2005 by Sheri Rose Shepherd
published by Multnomah Books

International Standard Book Number: 978-1-59052-470-1

Design by Koechel Peterson & Assoc, Inc, Minneapolis, Minnesota

Unless otherwise indicated, Scripture quotations are taken from: *The Amplified Bible* ©1965, 1987 by Zondervan Publishing House. Other Scripture quotations are from: *The Holy Bible,* New International Version (NIV) ©1973, 1984 by International Bible Society, used by permission of Zondervan Publishing House; *The Living Bible* (TLB) ©1971. Used by permission of Tyndale House Publishers, Inc. All rights reserved; *Holy Bible,* New Living Translation (NLT) ©1996. Used by permission of Tyndale House Publishers, Inc. All rights reserved; *New American Standard Bible* (NASB) ©1960, 1977 by the Lockman Foundation; *The Holy Bible,* New International Reader's Version (NIRV). Copyright ©1994, 1996 by International Bible Society. Used by permission of Zondervan Publishing House. All rights reserved; *Contemporary English Version* (CEV) ©1995 by American Bible Society.

Published in the United States by WaterBrook Multnomah, an imprint of the Crown Publishing Group, a division of Random House Inc., New York.

MULTNOMAH and its mountain colophon are registered trademarks of Random House Inc.

Printed in China

For Information:
MULTNOMAH BOOKS
12265 ORACLE BOULEVARD, SUITE 200
COLORADO SPRINGS, CO 80921

13—10 9 8 7

TABLE OF CONTENTS

Dear Princess,

I know from personal experience how hard it can be to feel close to God in prayer, to share with the Creator of heaven and earth your true feelings about life.

I used to think there was some magic formula. I spent years trying to say exactly the right things in just the right way. But then I read David's prayers in the Psalms, and I realized God wants me to express to Him my deepest fears, desires, and failures as well as my wholehearted love, praise, and thanksgiving. David's cries to God showed me that I can share my darkest secrets and my heartfelt joys. No topic or emotion is off limits to my King. He wants us to be *real* with Him! He loves us and He is the only One who can change our hearts or our circumstances.

So, as you read the prayers in this book, my prayer for you is that you will be reminded of your King's great power, His precious promises, and His immeasurable love for you. Even more, I am asking our King to use this book to encourage you to go confidently before His throne in prayer about *anything* because you are His princess and He cares about every detail of your life. He hears every word and is just waiting to bless you beyond imagination!

Love,
Your sister in Christ,
Sheri Rose

Now glory be to God who
by his mighty power at work within us
is able to do far more
than we would ever dare to ask or even dream of—
infinitely beyond our highest prayers,
desires, thoughts, or hopes.

EPHESIANS 3:20, TLB

You whom I have taken from the ends of the earth

and have called from the corners of it,

and said to you, You are My servant—

I have chosen you.

ISAIAH 41:9

My King,
WHO CHOSE ME

*I*t's so hard for me to believe that You *chose me* to represent You to the world.

Lord, I feel so inadequate to be called Your princess. I want to be what You've called me to be, but I don't know how. I need You to help me let go of who *I* think I am and become who *You* say I am. I know that You've given me a free will and that You would never force me to live for You, yet I want to be totally devoted to You. I want to leave a legacy with my life. I want the world to know I'm Yours. I'm asking You today to anoint me and show me how to live and act as Your princess. I'm choosing to believe that You will equip me to do everything You call me to do and keep me strong enough to finish my journey of faith. Thank You for embracing me as Your daughter and for loving me with Your life.

Because You first chose me…I choose to follow You today. I love You and I feel privileged to call You the Lord of my life and my Savior.

In Jesus' name, amen.

Love,

Your princess…who says "yes"

My King,

MY FATHER IN HEAVEN

I so desperately need to know Your fatherly love for me. I want to feel Your arms holding me when I hurt. I want to know Your wisdom when I have no idea what to do. I want to experience Your protection when I'm in danger and Your presence when I'm alone.

Please help me remember who You are and how much You love me. Don't ever let go of my hand as I walk through this journey called life. Remind me that I am safe in Your arms and that You are always there when I need to run to You. Let me never forget whose daughter I am. I long to love You not only as God, but as my Daddy in heaven.

In Jesus' name I pray.

Love,

Your daughter, who adores You

"AND I WILL BE YOUR FATHER,
AND YOU WILL BE MY SONS
AND DAUGHTERS, SAYS THE LORD ALMIGHTY."

2 CORINTHIANS 6:18, NLT

My King,

HELP ME FIND
MY IDENTITY IN YOU

*L*ord, set me free from trying to fit in to a world that so easily grabs hold of and twists my identity. I don't want to be molded any longer by man-made idols and human values. I want You to fashion my character and make me a reflection of You.

So, by Your Holy Spirit, warn me when I'm walking in the ways of the world and renew in me a heart that's right with You. Give me the passion to *bless* people so that I will stop wasting my life trying to merely *impress* them.

I believe that You can deliver me from the temptation to let others shape my identity and from my desire to please everyone around me. Lord, help me care more about what You think than what others think.

In Jesus' name, amen.

Love,

Your princess, who is grateful to be Yours

I will give thanks to You,

for I am fearfully and wonderfully made;

wonderful are Your works,

and my soul knows it very well.

PSALM 139:14, NASB

Return to the Lord, your God,
for He is gracious and merciful,
slow to anger,
and abounding in loving-kindness.

JOEL 2:13

My King,

TAKE ME BACK

Lord, I don't know how I wandered away from You again. I feel so lost when I'm not in tune to Your presence in my life.

I don't understand how one day I'm so on fire for Your love and the next day the embers of my faith seem to be smoldering and dying. Forgive me for straying from You. Forgive me for forgetting who You are and how much You love me and all that You've done for me.

I want to return to You. I want You to be the master of my mind and spirit. Let me feel Your Holy Spirit filling me up again. Bring me back into a right relationship with You again. I love You, and I am desperate for You. Please love me back to life again, because I'm hopeless without You. Thank You that You're *always* faithful, even when I'm not.

In Jesus' name, amen.

Love,

Your prodigal princess, who has come home

My King,
LET ME SHINE FOR YOU

*L*ord, Your Word says not to hide Your eternal light that is within me. And I do want others to know the hope You've given me. I want to have the boldness to burn brightly for You in this dark world.

So I ask You to help me not hide behind my fears of what others will think. Please shine Your light on those dark places in my heart that keep Your Holy Spirit from working through me. Make me into a star for You, a star that points people to heaven. Let my life reflect You in such a way that others will see Your lovingkindness, tenderness, and mercy and be drawn to You and You alone.

In Jesus' name I pray.

Love,

Your princess, who is ready to shine for You

"Arise, shine, for your light has come,

and the glory of the LORD rises upon you."

ISAIAH 60:1, NIV

THEREFORE THEN,
SINCE WE ARE SURROUNDED
BY SO GREAT A CLOUD OF WITNESSES,
LET US STRIP OFF AND THROW ASIDE
EVERY ENCUMBRANCE...
AND LET US RUN
WITH PATIENT ENDURANCE
AND STEADY AND ACTIVE PERSISTENCE
THE APPOINTED COURSE OF THE RACE
THAT IS SET BEFORE US.

HEBREWS 12:1

My King,
HELP ME RUN TO WIN

*L*ord, help me run in such a way that I will never tire of doing Your work. Be my heavenly coach. Train me physically, emotionally, and spiritually to win this race of faith. I will no longer run to compete with the world. I don't want any more worldly trophies that might glorify me. I want to run on Your team and win souls for Your kingdom. I run on an empty soul when I run for myself and in my own strength. You're the only One who can and will enable me to cross the finish line when this race is over. Starting today, I give You all that I am and all that I have, and I ask You to make me the person who wins the trophy of Your everlasting life.

In Jesus' name, amen.

Love,

Your princess, who's running toward the finish line

My King,
I WANT YOUR WAY

Lord, I've tried so many ways to make my life work. It feels like the more I try to have things my way, the further away from You I get. Help me to look up to You and not around me. Help me, God, to seek Your direction and hear Your voice when I'm lost and alone. Forgive me for not keeping my eyes on You. I know there is none like You, and no one could ever lead me or love me the way You do. I'm ready to follow You and You alone. So please put blinders on my eyes to the world and its ways, that I would stay on the straight and narrow path that leads me home to You.

In Jesus' name, amen.

Love,

Your princess, who loves where You lead

I guide you in the way of wisdom
and lead you along straight paths.

PROVERBS 4:11, NIV

I use God's mighty weapons,
not those made by men,
to knock down the devil's strongholds.
These weapons can break down
every proud argument against God
and every wall that can be built
to keep men from finding him.

2 CORINTHIANS 10:4–5, TLB

My King,
SET MY MIND ON YOU

*L*ord, sometimes I'm overwhelmed by the troubles in this world. I feel hopeless even though I know You are my hope. I feel inadequate to do anything significant that might help change all the crisis our nation is experiencing.

So I'm calling on You, Holy Spirit, to set my mind on the things I *can* do, on a daily basis, and on the people I *can* help, one at a time. Lift this spirit of oppression off of me; take my thoughts to a heavenly place where I can get an eternal view of Your plans and purposes. Renew my mind with Your truth and erase all doubt and discouragement. And help me remember that with You I am infinitely powerful to accomplish whatever is needed to make a difference for eternity.

In Jesus' name, amen.

Love,

Your princess, whose mind is on You

My King,

I NEED TO HEAR FROM YOU

My Lord, I let so many things drown out Your still small voice, things that don't make any difference in the story of my eternal life with You. Forgive me for the times I interrupt and even ignore You when You are wanting to speak to me. By Your Holy Spirit, convict me of the distractions I give in to and point out those people who take me away from You. Help me be quiet so that I can hear Your Spirit speak to me. Please help me be still and rest in Your Holy presence so that I might know what You are saying to me. Let Your Word penetrate my soul so deeply that it speaks louder than the world, so that I will recognize Your voice above all the chaos and busyness of my days.

In Jesus' name I pray.

Love,

Your princess, who is ready to listen

"Come to me with your ears wide open.
Listen, for the life of your soul is at stake.
I am ready to make an everlasting covenant with you.
I will give you all the mercies and
unfailing love that I promised to David."

ISAIAH 55:3, NLT

My King,
REMIND ME TO PRAY

Lord, I too easily forget how blessed I am to be able to enter into Your throne room with my prayers and problems. Thank You for this amazing privilege and gift. And prompt me, by Your Holy Spirit, to pray consistently and with confidence. Don't let me miss one divine touch from You because I have neglected to pray.

Remind me daily of whose daughter I am and how powerful You are. Help me to claim Your promises for me and for those I know and love. Help me to be Your princess warrior who binds Satan's schemes with the power of Your Word and my prayers.

Thank You that You always hear me call out to You. I praise You because You do more than listen—You answer faithfully according to Your perfect will. I feel privileged to pray. I love You, Lord, for who You are and all that You do.

In Jesus' name, amen.

Love,

Your princess, who is ready to pray

Pray at all times and on every occasion
in the power of the Holy Spirit.
Stay alert and be persistent in your prayers
for all Christians everywhere.

EPHESIANS 6:18, NLT

Don't be afraid, for I am with you.
Do not be dismayed, for I am your God. I will
strengthen you. I will help you. I will
uphold you with my victorious right hand.

ISAIAH 41:10, NLT

My King,

GIVE ME VICTORY

Jesus, I will never really know the price You paid on the cross so that I could live a life of victory. You willingly suffered the nails of the cross and a wrenching separation from Your heavenly Father—for *me*.

So when I'm overwhelmed by the pain and problems that come my way, remind me that You are God, my deliverer, my Savior, and my reason to live. Grant me victory over my fears. Open my eyes so I can see Your face instead of my fear. Let me find rest for my weary soul in Your presence. Make a way where there seems to be no way. Thank You that I am not alone. You are always with me and constantly working on my behalf. I praise You that I can be victorious in every area of my life because I am Yours.

In Your name, amen.

Love,

Your princess, who will triumph through this trial

Do you not know that your body is the temple

of the Holy Spirit

Who lives within you,

Whom you have received [as a Gift] from God?

You are not your own.

1 CORINTHIANS 6:19

My King,
KEEP ME PURE

*L*ord, help me to remember that my body is the dwelling place of Your Holy Spirit. Keep me strong in Your truth and in Your ways. I don't want to dishonor Your temple by defiling what is Yours. I know my body is not my own: You paid with Your life the price of my salvation.

I can't begin to tell You how much I value this precious gift from You, yet sometimes it's hard for me to see myself as precious or valuable. Please renew my mind with Your truth, hold on to my heart with Your love, and grab hold of my worldly convictions and make them Yours.

I need You to help me stay pure. I want Your wisdom and Your strength to walk away from anyone or anything that would tempt me to compromise who I am destined to be—Your child, set apart and made holy for Your purposes.

In Jesus' name, amen.

Love,

Your princess, who will love You always

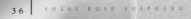

If we admit that we have
sinned and confess our sins,
He is faithful and just and will forgive our sins
and cleanse us from all unrighteousness.

1 JOHN 1:9

My King,
PLEASE FORGIVE ME

*L*ord, please forgive me for sinning against You. I so need Your healing touch right now because I have failed once again to be the person You want me to be, and I am struggling to forgive myself. I need You to wash me as white as snow and to cover my past mistakes with Your blood. I want to start over. I'm ready to walk away from my old life and become a new person. But there's no way I can do this by myself. I'm lost without You, Jesus. So please, right now, send Your Holy Spirit to show me what I need to do to get right with You, and to make things right with others. I thank You, Lord, that You are the God of second chances. I thank You that once I repent, You never see my sin again. Thank You that I'm forgiven because You were forsaken.

In Your name, amen.

Love,

Your princess, who has returned to You

My King,

YOU ARE MY REWARD

*L*ord, You are my true treasure and reward in life. Yet the rewards which the world offers—the praise of people, the approval of others, even my pride—can too easily well up within and distract me. I want to let You have all the praise for anything I've done. I want what I do to glorify my King…You. My reward is Your amazing presence in my life.

I am ready to store up heavenly rewards and eternal treasures. Never let me forget the greatest reward of all is spending eternity with You. Forgive me for trying to reward myself and forgive me for investing in the "here and now" rather than in Your kingdom, which will last forever. It's a great honor and treasure just to be called Your daughter. Thank You for all the extra blessings You bestow on me.

In Jesus' name, amen.

Love,

Your princess, who treasures You

For the Son of Man is going to come
in the glory of His Father with His angels,
and then He will render account
and reward every man
in accordance with what he has done.

MATTHEW 16:27

My King,

PLEASE LEAD THE WAY

*L*ord, I want You to be my guide; I need Your divine direction. Yet so many times I wander off the narrow road You paved for me with Your life. Somehow I can feel that my way is better than Your will for me, that my fun is more important to me than my faith. I forget that You, my Father, know what's best for me. So when I wander away from You, let me hear Your Holy Spirit whisper, "Follow Me, I am the Way." Let me know Your direction for my life.

I'm ready to let You lead me. I'm ready to walk with You through Your Word, one step at a time. I want to stay on the road that leads me to You every day, every minute, until I'm with You on the other side of eternity.

In Jesus' name, amen.

Love,

Your princess, who needs and wants Your guidance

BUT THANKS BE TO GOD, WHO ALWAYS
LEADS US IN TRIUMPHAL PROCESSION IN CHRIST
AND THROUGH US SPREADS EVERYWHERE
THE FRAGRANCE OF THE KNOWLEDGE OF HIM.

2 CORINTHIANS 2:14, NIV

My King,
PLEASE MAKE ME BEAUTIFUL

Lord, I waste so much time trying to make myself beautiful to others. I want my character to reflect Your beauty. Deliver me from trying to fashion who I am based on the world's standards. Let me look to You to be my mirror, my master makeup artist. Line my lips with words of life and make up my eyes with compassion. Cover my imperfections with Your grace and my insecurities with security in You. Who can embellish me better than You? No one can make me more attractive to others than Your spirit can within me. I praise You for creating me in Your image and for continuing to re-create me to be more like You. Every day I seek You, I'm asking You for a complete spiritual makeover...so when people look at me they see Your beauty, Your love, and Your irresistible gift of salvation.

In Jesus' name I pray.

Love,

Your princess, who longs to reflect Your beauty

*Don't be concerned about
the outward beauty that depends on jewelry,
or beautiful clothes, or hair arrangement.
Be beautiful inside, in your hearts,
with the lasting charm of a gentle
and quiet spirit which is so precious to God.*

1 PETER 3:3–4, TLB

NO ONE WILL BE ABLE
TO STAND UP AGAINST YOU
ALL THE DAYS OF YOUR LIFE.
AS I WAS WITH MOSES,
SO I WILL BE WITH YOU;
I WILL NEVER LEAVE YOU
NOR FORSAKE YOU.

JOSHUA 1:5, NIV

My King,
WHO IS WITH ME ALWAYS

Lord, Your Word promises You are always with me. But sometimes I still feel so alone in this world. Please let me know that You are with me everywhere I go. Let me find comfort in knowing that You are everything to me—my strength when I am weak, my shield, my friend, my Father and King. Forgive me for doubting Your holy presence in my life. Help me to know that You can fill that empty void whenever I call to You. Help me to remember I am never alone because the God of heaven and earth resides inside of me and loves me more than I can ever imagine. Thank You that You will never leave me or forsake me. Thank You for being the friend that walks in when the world walks out. I am so grateful that You are my God and that I have a precious relationship with You.

In Jesus' name, amen.

Love,

Your princess, who is grateful that You are here

My King,

MAY I FIND FREEDOM IN YOU

Lord, Your Word says I am free because I am Yours, but sometimes I don't feel free. You know those hidden places in my heart that keep me locked up in a private prison cell of pain. I am desperate for You to shine Your light of hope and healing into my dark and painful places. I need You to teach me the keys to freedom that are hidden in Your Word. Bless my obedience and lead me out of captivity into true freedom. Give me the courage to let You unlock the chains holding me hostage. I choose this day to walk out of my dark and lonely private pain and step out in faith to walk in freedom. I will break away from any and all things that are not part of Your perfect will for my life, and I will believe Your promise to be true. He who the Son has set free is free indeed!

In Jesus' name I pray.

Love,

Your princess, who is ready to be free

Now the Lord is the Spirit,
and where the Spirit of the Lord is,
there is liberty.

2 CORINTHIANS 3:17

For I know the one in whom I trust,
and I am sure that he is able
to safely guard all that I have given him
until the day of his return.

2 TIMOTHY 1:12, TLB

My King,
I ENTRUST THOSE
I LOVE TO YOUR CARE

Lord, I so desperately want to let go of my fears and worries about those I love. I often find myself afraid for their future, their health, and their safety. I don't want to see them hurt or suffer. Yet I know that You didn't call me to protect those I love through fear, but by faith and prayer. So please, God, help me remember that You love my family and friends more than I do. Help me to rest in the fact that they belong to You and You alone. When hard things happen to those I love, help me trust Your promise to work all things together for good for those who are Yours. I choose right now to trade my fear for faith in Your love and protection over their lives.

In Jesus' name I pray.

Love,

Your princess, who releases my loved ones to You

My King,
YOU ARE MY REDEEMER

*L*ord, sometimes I look back on my life and regret the days I wasted by not living for You. I let so many circumstances interfere with our love relationship. I let people and pain keep me paralyzed, unable to live as Your princess. I'm so grateful that You can take whatever I give You now, and whatever time I have left here on earth, and use it for Your kingdom. I'm glad You can use me to finish the work You set out for me to do from the beginning of time. And I praise You for being able to redeem the days that were lost, Lord. Help me let go of what's gone wrong and cling to the future with hope in You and a heart filled with the joy of my salvation.

In Jesus' name I pray.

Love,

Your princess, who finds hope in You

But now, this is what the LORD says....
"Fear not, for I have redeemed you;
I have summoned you by name;
you are mine."

ISAIAH 43:1, NIV

My King,
MY COMMANDER IN BATTLE

*L*ord, help me to remember as I face life's challenges that an unseen spiritual war is going on and that my real battles are not with people, but against the enemy's darkness. Send Your Holy Spirit to give me the wisdom to know what issues are worth fighting for; teach me to walk away from meaningless battles; and remind me that the best way to win the battles in my life is on my knees in prayer. I'm tired of fighting in my own strength—and losing ground to Satan. I'm ready to let You be the commander of my life and have You bring the victory I'm so desperate to know. I surrender all to You today and let You fight for me. If You are with me, I know *nothing* can destroy me. Thank You for being my hero.

In Jesus' name I pray.

Love,

Your princess, who loves that You fight for Your children

"Not by might nor by power,
but by my Spirit,"
says the LORD Almighty.

ZECHARIAH 4:6, NIV

God has given gifts to each of you
from his great variety of spiritual gifts.
Manage them well so that God's generosity
can flow through you.

1 PETER 4:10, NLT

My King,
WHO'S GIVEN ME GIFTS

Lord, I want my life to be a gift to all I know and love. I need You to help me overcome my insecurities and allow You to unwrap the person You created me to be. Show me how to serve others. I want to be a blessing, not a burden. Show me what my gifts are and how to give them away. Forgive me for using the gifts I *do* know I have to bring glory to myself and not You. Forgive me for spending so much energy trying to impress others instead of trying to bless them with what I have been given by You. Today I want to give You a gift. I want to give You all that I am and all that I have to use for the world You love so much and died for. Thank You for loving me with Your life and giving me the gift of my salvation.

In Jesus' name I pray.

Love,

Your princess, who wants to use her gifts

The LORD is my strength and my song;

he has become my salvation.

He is my God, and I will praise him.

EXODUS 15:2, NIV

My King,

YOU ARE THE SONG OF MY LIFE

Lord God, I love the fact that You have written the music of my life. You have placed every note so I can hear Your beautiful Spirit whisper sweet songs to me. I love to sense Your presence when I praise and worship You with songs of love. Thank You that, by Your Spirit, You put a song of joy in my life and the peace of heaven inside of me. I'm thankful for the eternal composition You have arranged just for me that is being played out through my life each day. Let me never be deaf to Your beautiful music of love. May my heart always be full of the heavenly music of love You have written just for me.

In Jesus' name, amen.

Love,

Your princess, who loves Your heavenly melodies

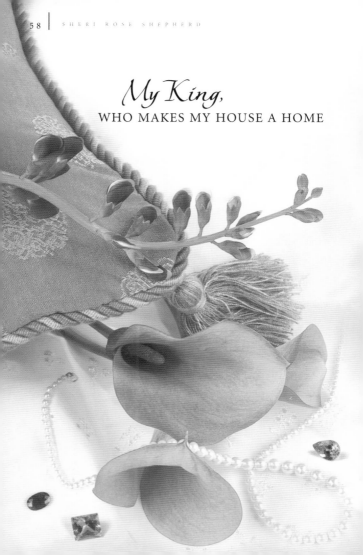

My King,
WHO MAKES MY HOUSE A HOME

*L*ord, You know me, and You know how much I want my home to be perfect in every way. I want to decorate and surround myself with beautiful accessories and furnishings. And I know You love to bless me, but help me care more about Your presence in my home than about the decor. Forgive me for the times I've made my family and friends feel that the things in my home are more valuable than the people I love most. Show me how to care more about the people in my home than about the things I own. Help me make my home a safe haven in a harsh world. Fill my house with Your love and peace as I fill it with music of praise to You. Give me a heart that longs to serve and that helps my family feel loved and cared for.

In Jesus' name, amen.

Love,

Your princess, who loves how You decorate my life

JESUS REPLIED, "IF ANYONE LOVES ME,
HE WILL OBEY MY TEACHING.
MY FATHER WILL LOVE HIM,
AND WE WILL COME TO HIM
AND MAKE OUR HOME WITH HIM."

JOHN 14:23, NIV

My King,

LET ME BE YOUR HANDS

Lord, teach me how to reach out with Your love to those in need. Give me eyes to see those who are hurting, a heart to help them, and the strength to do whatever You would have me do. Use me to do Your work in this world. Please guide me and bless all that I set out to do each time You call me to love my neighbor.

As You and I work together, let me never forget that it is You working through me that accomplishes Your will. Apart from You I can do nothing. So I ask You, Holy Spirit, to anoint my hands and use them for Your kingdom work in the lives of people I know.

In Jesus' name, amen.

Love,

Your princess, whose hands are ready to be used

For the LORD your God will bless you in

all your harvest and in

all the work of your hands,

and your joy will be complete.

DEUTERONOMY 16:15, NIV

Set a guard over my mouth, O LORD;
keep watch over the door of my lips.

PSALM 141:3, NIV

My King,
ANOINT MY MOUTH

Lord, I am very aware of the damage I can too easily do with the words I speak. The power of life and death is indeed in my tongue, and too often I choose to speak words of death. Forgive me for using my words to condemn instead of to comfort…to hurt rather than to heal…and to bring others down when I could instead choose to build them up.

Like King David, I am asking You to guard what I say. Send Your Holy Spirit to convict me before I speak words that would not be pleasing in Your sight. Teach me to speak like the princess You called me to be, and bring words of healing to those I have hurt in my careless conversations.

In Jesus' name, amen.

Love,

Your princess, who longs to speak graciously

My King,

WHO IS MY CONFIDENCE

Lord, I feel as if I'm on a roller coaster. One moment I'm walking tall and believing what You say about me—that I'm fearfully and wonderfully made—and the next moment I'm screaming on the inside for people's approval. I'm asking You to reveal the root cause of my insecurity and to teach me to walk through this life in Your truth and power—not just *some* of the time, but *all* of the time. I don't want to ride through life in a seat of self-defeat, stuck in the rut of people's opinions. I want to keep my eyes on You; I want to live for You and Your approval alone. I want to live with confidence as Your redeemed daughter and cherished princess.

In Jesus' name, amen.

Love,

Your princess, who finds confidence and power in You

For God did not give us a spirit of timidity,
but of power and of love
and of calm and well-balanced mind.

2 TIMOTHY 1:7

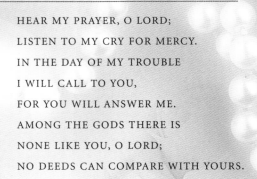

HEAR MY PRAYER, O LORD;

LISTEN TO MY CRY FOR MERCY.

IN THE DAY OF MY TROUBLE

I WILL CALL TO YOU,

FOR YOU WILL ANSWER ME.

AMONG THE GODS THERE IS

NONE LIKE YOU, O LORD;

NO DEEDS CAN COMPARE WITH YOURS.

PSALM 86:6–8, NIV

My King,
PLEASE PROTECT ME

*L*ord, I know there are spiritual battles raging around me; sometimes I feel so afraid. Help me to trust You, my God, more than I fear the attacks of Satan. Let me cling to Your Word and to the truth that greater is Your Spirit who is in me than the enemy and his dark forces which prowl all around me. I don't want to live in fear.

Remind me to run to You, my Fortress, when I need protection. I cannot fight this battle alone. I choose by faith to trust that You can and will take care of me and all that is attacking my life. I love You, almighty God, for Your protection and provision. You are amazing to me. I am blessed to rest in You.

In Jesus' name, amen.

Love,

Your princess, who finds peace in Your protection

My King,
KEEP ME FROM COMPROMISE

Lord, keep me strong in my commitment to You. Help me to walk away from worldly temptations. I don't want to be defeated in the enemy's war for my soul. Keep me alert to his attacks. Let me live in a way that is distinct from the world. Help me resist the temptation to seize one moment of worldly pleasure only to find a lifetime of regret. Prompt me to look to You when I need a way of escape because You promise in Your Word You'll always provide a way out for Your children when we're tempted. Send Your Spirit to convict me of sin and put in my heart a desire to be obedient to Your Word. And please forgive me for those times I let temptation turn me away from You. I love You and I long to do what is right in Your sight.

In Jesus' name, amen.

Love,

Your princess, who needs Your strength to walk in Your ways

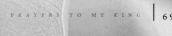

Keep awake and watch and pray,
that you may not enter into temptation;
the spirit indeed is willing, but the flesh is weak.

MARK 14:38

And I pray that Christ will be more and more
at home in your hearts, living within you
as you trust in him.
May your roots go down deep
into the soil of God's marvelous love....

EPHESIANS 3:17, TLB

My King,
MY MASTER GARDENER

Lord, help me to serve You right where You have placed me in life. Help me to stop putting off what You have called me to do. I want to love You with all that I am, love the people You have put in my life, and share my faith with others.

I know my tendency to want to wait for the "perfect" place and time in life to do something grand for You. Forgive me for making excuses for not living for You *today*. I know that life will never be perfect until I am home in heaven with You and I know that it is in the imperfect world that Your love needs to be shared.

So I am asking You to prune me and water me with Your Word so that I will grow into the woman You want me to be. Use me to sow seeds of faith in the lives of others just as You used others to plant the same seeds in me.

In Jesus' name, amen.

Love,

Your princess, who wants to grow and help others grow, too

My King,
WHOSE TIMING IS PERFECT

*L*ord, I know in my heart that Your timing is perfect, but I still feel restless in my spirit as I wait. I want to see Your plans for my life unfold *now*. I want to know ahead of time what the future holds for me. It is so hard for me not to try to control circumstances or manipulate situations so that things happen the way *I* want and according to *my* time frame.

So, during this season of waiting, carve into my character all I will need to fulfill Your amazing plans for my life. Don't let me waste my time while I wait on You. Grant me Your perfect peace while You prepare me. Give me wisdom about when to move and when to be still. Remind me daily that Your timing is perfect and that Your plan is for my everlasting good.

In Jesus' name, amen.

Love,

Your princess, who chooses to wait on

Your timing

There is a proper time and procedure
for every matter,
though a man's misery weighs heavily upon him.

ECCLESIASTES 8:6, NIV

My King,
HEAL MY HEART

*L*ord, I need to feel Your healing touch. This is one of those times when I am paralyzed by heartache. I don't know how to deal with my pain and disappointment; I don't know how I can be healed from my wounds. But I do know to turn to You.

Lord, I'm desperate for You, so please help me rest in Your holy and healing presence. As I do, touch me with Your tender hand that brings a renewed spirit and wholeness. Give me the strength I need to cling to You when I feel like running away.

I know the enemy wants to defeat me, especially when I am down. So please help me to stay strong in my faith and trust that You can and will restore to me the joy of my salvation. Begin to heal me now and bring back my hope and peace of mind.

In Jesus' name, amen.

Love,

Your princess, who is longing to be whole

He heals the brokenhearted,
binding up their wounds.
How great is our Lord! His power is absolute!
His understanding is beyond comprehension!

PSALM 147:3, 5, NLT

HAVE I NOT COMMANDED YOU?
BE STRONG, VIGOROUS, AND VERY COURAGEOUS.
BE NOT AFRAID, NEITHER BE DISMAYED,
FOR THE LORD YOUR GOD IS WITH YOU
WHEREVER YOU GO.

JOSHUA 1:9

My King,
GRANT ME COURAGE

*L*ord, grant me the courage I need to stand against the enemy of my soul, the courage to do what is right in Your sight. I need the same kind of courage that You gave young David when he faced Goliath, courage rooted in my trust in You. Give me a faith that will enable me to defeat any giant that tries to interfere with Your perfect plan for my life. Help me stand firm no matter how big the enemy may seem.

I know, Lord, how weak I am when I try to stand in my own strength. I am very aware that I need Your shield of faith, the breastplate of Your righteousness, the belt of Your truth, and the power of Your Holy Spirit. Thank You for giving me all that I need to be strong in You and courageous for You.

In Jesus' name, amen.

Love,

Your princess, who wants to be strong in You

"For God so loved the world
that he gave his one and only Son,
that whoever believes in him shall not perish
but have eternal life.
For God did not send his Son
into the world to condemn the world,
but to save the world through him."

JOHN 3:16–17, NIV

My King,
YOU SENT YOUR SON FOR ME

*L*ord God, it's so amazing that You sent Jesus, Your only Son, to die for me. I can hardly fathom that You, who created the heavens and the earth, sent Your only Son to give me abundant life, peace with the Almighty, and the freedom to pray to You. I have received so much, all because Jesus my Savior was rejected, persecuted, killed, and forsaken. Lord God, Your love overwhelms me. Please forgive me when I take for granted this immeasurable sacrificial gift. Forgive me for the times when I care more about serving myself than serving You. Let me never forget the price my Jesus paid for me personally—letting me live for You alone.

In Jesus' name, amen.

Love,

Your princess, who's glad You sent Jesus for me

My King,
WHO WALKS WITH ME

*L*ord, I love walking through life with You. The places You take me fill me with peace, purpose, and joy. I know Your way is always the right way.

Yet so many times I want to walk in the ways of the world. I want to experience the excitement of life. There is a real struggle in my soul. One part of me longs to never wander off Your road of everlasting life, but the other part too easily travels down the road of worldly pleasures and self-destruction.

Yet still You love me. And I am amazed by how many times You come find me when I lose my way. How faithful You are to me no matter how many times I walk away from You. So here I am again, asking for my heavenly Father's forgiveness and divine direction back to the road that leads me home to You.

In Jesus' name, amen.

Love,

Your princess, who wants to walk every step with You

> I AM THE LIGHT OF THE WORLD.
> HE WHO FOLLOWS ME WILL NOT BE
> WALKING IN THE DARK,
> BUT WILL HAVE THE LIGHT WHICH IS LIFE.
>
> JOHN 8:12

My King,
MY DIVINE DRESSER

Lord, my heart feels burdened when I look at the wardrobes of this world and how women will wear anything to get attention and feel valued. Yet I confess I'm guilty of wearing some of them myself! Please help me stop conforming to this world: I don't want to be defined by a fashion designer any longer.

Lord, convict me of the clothes in my closet that make me look like someone other than Your princess. Set me free from being a slave to the world's fashions and clothe me instead with the attributes of my Savior. Then use me to set the trends of holiness and purity.

From now on, may whatever I wear reflect my commitment to You. Use my identity in You to touch the hearts of people all around me. I want to represent You in fashions of Your heavenly creation rather than in the ungodly trends this world offers.

I'm ready to be Your model of life to everyone around me.

In Jesus' name, amen.

Love,

Your princess, who wants to dress for You

I will greatly rejoice in the Lord,
my soul will exult in my God;
for He has clothed me with the garments of salvation,
He has covered me with the robe of righteousness...
as a bride adorns herself with her jewels.

ISAIAH 61:10

"I am leaving you with a gift—
peace of mind and heart.
And the peace I give isn't like the
peace the world gives.
So don't be troubled or afraid."

JOHN 14:27, NLT

My King,
WHO WIPES AWAY MY FEARS

*L*ord, whenever I am afraid, help me trust You. Transform my fear, whatever its cause, into faith in You.

Lord, it seems like there are many reasons to fear, and I am sometimes overwhelmed. By fear of disaster, fear of my financial future, and fear of sickness. I fear for my family and my friends, my job and my life. The list seems endless!

Yet I know You don't want me to live a life driven by fear. You want me to rest in You. Remind me whose hand of protection is all around me. Keep me in Your perfect peace. When my mind is spiraling out of control with concerns, give me the ability to turn from being a problem worrier to being a prayer warrior. Let me walk through life knowing Your perfect peace, no matter what is happening around me.

In Jesus' name, amen.

Love,

Your princess, who is choosing trust in You over fear

My King,
YOU ARE TRUTH

*L*ord, let Your truth drown out the world's lies about who I am supposed to be. I never want to forget the day that I asked You to be my Lord and Savior…the day I became a daughter of the King, Your princess. I praise You that my name is written in Your book of everlasting life. How blessed I am to be called by You!

Thank You that Your truth exposes the lies of Satan and that Your Word is the ultimate and unchangeable authority for my life. Help me to stand on Your Word whenever I feel worthless, help me to accept Your perfect love whenever I feel rejected, and help me to find my confidence in You whenever I feel insecure.

Write on my heart the truth I read in my Bible about who I am, how much I am loved, and why I'm really here…to glorify You, my God.

In Jesus' name, amen.

Love,

Your princess, who cherishes Your truth

And now you also have heard the truth,
the Good News that God saves you.
And when you believed in Christ,
he identified you as his own
by giving you the Holy Spirit,
whom he promised long ago.

EPHESIANS 1:13, NLT

YOU WILL KEEP IN PERFECT PEACE
HIM WHOSE MIND IS STEADFAST,
BECAUSE HE TRUSTS IN YOU.

ISAIAH 26:3, NIV

My King,

YOU ARE MY PERFECT PEACE

*L*ord, thank You for the perfect peace I can know in You, a peace that passes all human understanding. I am so blessed to know You personally and to live a life of peace in this world of confusion and chaos.

I love You for all the times You have carried me through troubles that could have overwhelmed me. And I love You for those times when I have cried out to You and You have answered. Thank You for those times that I thought there was no way and You made a way. I praise You for Your amazing peace.

Lord God, the next time my peace is broken by problems that come, remind me that You are always there caring about anything and everything that concerns me. I want to praise You through the painful places I walk through so I can rest in Your perfect peace.

In Jesus' name, amen.

Love,

Your princess, whose heart finds rest in You

My King,

I WANT TO RUN TO YOUR ARMS

Lord, I've been running to everyone and everything but You. All the while You have been watching, waiting, and wanting me to run to You. Please forgive me for ignoring Your gentle call to me. I don't know why it's so hard for me to go first to You. No one can handle me or my issues in life better than You. I'm sorry, Lord, for choosing other things—other relationships, other activities, other interests—over You.

Lord, I so need You now. I want to spend time with You again. I'm ready to choose Your love over my love for the world. I want You to be the one I run to when I'm celebrating, crying, or in a crisis, so I'm coming back to You now.

Thank You that Your arms are always open wide for Your daughter. Thank You that You never turn Your back on me. How blessed I am to have a Daddy who's never too busy for me, never absent, and always wants to hold me.

In Jesus' name, amen.

Love,

Your princess, who wants to be near You

The eternal God is your refuge
and dwelling place,
and underneath are the everlasting arms.

DEUTERONOMY 33:27

He will be the sure foundation for your times,
a rich store of salvation and wisdom and knowledge;
the fear of the LORD is the key to this treasure.

ISAIAH 33:6, NIV

My God,
YOU ARE MY ETERNAL TREASURE

*L*ord, help me set my eyes on the eternal treasures that You have stored up for me in heaven. Deliver me from my senseless efforts to store up worldly things that won't last. You know how I struggle daily with wanting more, believing that I need more, and working for more, but then I enter Your presence and realize that my true treasure is You.

I remember Your truth says that I came into this world with nothing, and that I'll leave with nothing. I remember Your promise about rewards You are waiting to give me when I enter Your Kingdom—my eternal home. Give me a heart that longs to store up treasures in heaven. Let me live for the day when we will see each other face-to-face. What a treasure that precious day will be!

In Jesus' name, amen.

Love,

Your princess, who treasures You

My King,
MY BRIDEGROOM

Lord, I'm so looking forward to that great day when we will celebrate, in heaven, the great wedding feast that You have personally prepared for me. Help me to remember that I am a bride of Christ. Give me what I need to prepare for my eternal wedding day when I will be presented to You. Hold the key to my heart and keep me ever faithful as I wait for that wonderful day. Dress me in Your righteousness and present me pure and holy. Help me to do all I can to be the bride You desire me to be. Let me never forget my first love is You!

In Jesus' precious name, amen.

Love,

Your princess, Your bride-to-be

"Let us be glad and rejoice
and honor him; for the time has come
for the wedding banquet of the Lamb,
and his bride has prepared herself.
She is permitted to wear
the cleanest and whitest and finest of linens."

REVELATION 19:7–8, TLB

My King,

SET ME FREE TO LOVE OTHERS

Lord, You ask me to love others and I want to love others the way You love me—freely and generously, with no thought of what I'll receive in return. But I'm so afraid that I'll get hurt. Please free me from my fear of rejection. Please give me the ability to love people the most, even when they deserve it the least. Show me when to stay and when to walk away. Help me give my love…*unconditionally.* And keep me so close to You that I don't need to be filled up by anyone but You. I want You to be my first love. I want Your Spirit to fill me up to overflowing so that I can share You with a world that is desperate to be loved and valued.

In Jesus' name, amen.

Love,

Your princess, who wants to spread Your love

Jesus replied: "'Love the Lord your God
with all your heart and with all your soul
and with all your mind.'
"And the second is like it:
'Love your neighbor as yourself.'"

MATTHEW 22:37, 39, NIV

"For I know the plans I have for you,"
declares the LORD, *"plans to prosper you*
and not to harm you, plans to give you
hope and a future."

JEREMIAH 29:11, NIV

My God,

SHOW ME YOUR PLANS FOR ME

*L*ord, I want to do so many things with my life, and I long to see my dreams come true. But there are so many times when I don't come to You with my hopes and dreams. I don't pray for Your perfect plan.

Please forgive me when I forget that You are God and I am not; forgive me when I forget that I have named You Lord of my life yet I try and act as lord. Remind me that Your ways are better than my ways. Convict me when I plan this life that You gave me without involving You.

Today I give You my plans, my ideas, my dreams, and my goals, and I'm asking You, my Father, to show me what You want me to do with my life. Help me to keep my eyes on You. You can do more than I would ever dare to dream or even ask for. I want Your way and Your perfect will.

In Jesus' name I pray.

Love,

Your princess, who wants to do Your will

The LORD answered,
"I can do anything!
Watch and you'll see my words
come true."

NUMBERS 11:23, CEV

My King,
WITH YOU I CAN DO ANYTHING

*L*ord, I so want to see Your power displayed in my life. Your Word says that nothing is too big for You to handle, that *nothing* is impossible for You!

But Lord, I struggle with believing that Your promises are for me personally. I want to be a woman of faith, a woman who trusts You in every situation. Please make the truth and power of Your Word more real to me.

Lord, please give me the ability to do the good works You have planned for me. Help me not to miss one opportunity to serve You and Your people; help me not to miss one miracle that You do in my life and the lives of those around me. And, Lord, let my life reflect to the world that You are the King of kings and the God of miracles.

In Jesus' name, amen.

Love,

Your princess, who calls on Your power

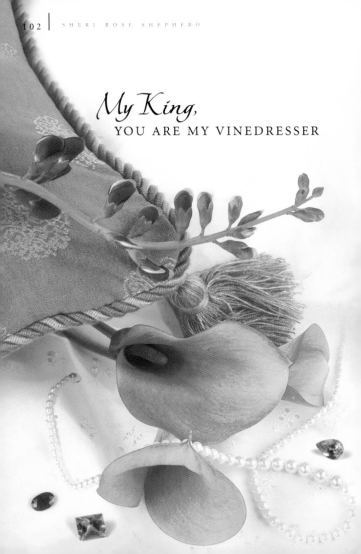

My King,
YOU ARE MY VINEDRESSER

*L*ord, I am so grateful to be eternally connected to You. I know that apart from You I can't do anything that really matters. So please show me how to *stay* connected to You.

Help me to let You be the gardener of my life. Sometimes when You prune me, I feel angry and resistant. I want You to grow me into the person that You designed me to be, I want to be fruitful and live a life of integrity. So remind me that my character is more important than my comfort. And that as I stay true to You, let Your love go down deep into the soil of my soul and continue to grow me into the woman I long to become, a true daughter of the King. *Your* daughter!

In Jesus' name, amen.

Love,

Your princess, who wants to bear fruit for Your Kingdom

I AM THE TRUE VINE,
AND MY FATHER IS THE VINEDRESSER.
...HE CLEANSES AND REPEATEDLY PRUNES EVERY BRANCH
THAT CONTINUES TO BEAR FRUIT,
TO MAKE IT BEAR MORE AND RICHER
AND MORE EXCELLENT FRUIT.
JOHN 15:1–2

My God,
MY BEST FRIEND

*L*ord, I love You. You truly are my very best friend. You fill me up when I feel empty and alone. You comfort me when I cry. You take care of me like no one else can. You know me and my downfalls better than anyone else, yet You still love me.

And I know that You are with me wherever I am. How *blessed* I am to be accompanied by the Creator of the heavens and the earth as I journey through this life.

Never let me forget that You are with me always even until the end of time. Engrave in my mind the memories of those times You have loved me when I was unlovable and all those times You forgave me when I sinned against You. Let me never forget where I was when I met You, and how far You've brought me in life.

Thank You for forgiving my sins. Thank You for Your constant presence with me. Thank You for being my faithful Friend who will never leave me nor forsake me.

In Jesus' name, amen.

Love,

Your princess, who loves You more every day

"Lord, you are the God of heaven.
You are a great and wonderful God.
You keep the covenant you made
with those who love you and obey your commands.
You show them your love."

NEHEMIAH 1:5, NIRV

The LORD gives sight to the blind,
the LORD lifts up those who are bowed down,
the LORD loves the righteous.

PSALM 146:8, NIV

My God,
WHO GIVES ME SIGHT

*L*ord, open my spiritual eyes so that I can see with an eternal point of view what matters most to You. Let me see the beauty of Your creation all around me. Let me recognize the divine appointments You have set for me. Let me see the people I meet as those You love and died for.

Help me to get my eyes off of my circumstances and back onto You. I don't want to be blinded any longer by the pain and problems in my life. I don't want to lose my spiritual sight by the lies Satan tries to put in my mind. I know that I need to look to You and Your truth to be a lamp unto my feet and a light when I feel like I'm in the dark.

Lord, You gave me sight when You created me, and now I ask You to give me supernatural vision to see the world the way You see it, and then the supernatural strength to serve in it as You serve me.

In Jesus' name I pray.

Love,

Your princess, who wants to see as You see

My King,
GUARD MY MIND

Lord, I want my mind to be set on You, but I struggle every day with choosing between what I know is right and what I want to do. Sometimes I find it so hard to walk away from worldly pleasures, even though I know that what I am reading, watching, or listening to represents everything that I don't want to be or be part of.

Give me deep convictions to live in a way that honors You. Renew my mind as I read Your Word. Show me when I'm careless to pollute my own mind in the name of recreation or relaxation.

I don't want to be half Yours and half the world's any longer. I want to be *all* Yours. Show me those things I allow into my mind that keep me from You and that interfere with Your plans for me. And then give me the strength to turn from them and once again to keep my mind set on You.

In Jesus' name, amen.

Love,

Your princess, who sets her mind on You

Do not be conformed to this world,
but be transformed by the renewal of your mind,
so that you may prove what is the good
and acceptable
and perfect will of God.

ROMANS 12:2

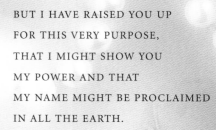

BUT I HAVE RAISED YOU UP
FOR THIS VERY PURPOSE,
THAT I MIGHT SHOW YOU
MY POWER AND THAT
MY NAME MIGHT BE PROCLAIMED
IN ALL THE EARTH.

EXODUS 9:16, NIV

My King,
UPHOLD MY ROYAL PURPOSE

*L*ord, I long to be lifted up to a place of influence for You. I want my life to make a difference for Your kingdom. So I am asking You to prepare me for my royal calling and to guide my steps toward Your purpose.

I am ready to give up whatever is necessary so that I will take a stand for the name that is above all names—*Jesus*. I admit, though, that I don't exactly know where to start or even how to live as Your princess. But I do know that as I seek You, I trust You will show me the way and give me all that I need to complete the royal call You have on my life.

So, just as You did for Queen Esther, I ask You to use me in a mighty way for such a time as this.

In Jesus' name I pray.

Love,

Your princess, who is ready to be used by You

My God,

TEACH ME TO PRAY

Lord, I want to learn to pray with power. I want to do *more* than cry out to You for personal needs. I'm Your daughter. I want to be in constant communion with You, and I want to be a woman who prays with purpose and divine intervention.

So I ask You to quicken my spirit and show me how to pray. Prompt me to intercede boldly and vigorously for others. Remind me to approach Your throne with confidence and consistency. I don't want the devil to destroy anyone or gain ground in this world when You have given me power, in the name of Jesus, to pray. Forgive me for the times I have neglected to pray or walked away from the privilege and the responsibility of prayer.

I'm ready to be a princess prayer warrior for You.

In Jesus' name, amen.

Love,

The princess You love and who is ready to pray

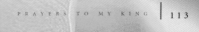

Pray at all times and on every occasion
in the power of the Holy Spirit.
Stay alert and be persistent in your prayers
for all Christians everywhere.

EPHESIANS 6:18, NLT

At midnight I will rise to give thanks to You

because of Your righteous ordinances.

I am a companion of all those who fear,

revere, and worship You,

and of those who observe and give heed to Your precepts.

PSALM 119:62–63

My God,
CHOOSE MY FRIENDS

*L*ord, my relationships are so different from what I want them to be. Help me become the kind of friend I long to have. Help me to invest my time in the people You know I need in my life. I'm asking You to choose my friends for me.

Give me wisdom about when to work through my differences with people and when to walk away. Give me a heart that tunes in to the needs of those people whom I love. Forgive me when I make friendships all about me. I want to develop intimate relationships, ordained and blessed by You, where we can encourage and nurture each other to be our best for You. You are the truest friend ever. Let me experience royal relationships ordained by You.

In Jesus' name, amen.

Love,

Your princess, who longs to be a good friend

My King,
MY KEY TO FREEDOM

Lord, I need You to set me free. Even though I have tasted the fruit of Your freedom at times in my life, there are certain things and certain people in my private world that cause me to feel bound up by heavy chains of pain and discomfort. I am desperate for You to give me the courage and faith to demolish the chains that weigh me down with shame, regret, guilt, and anger. I want to break free to the *victorious* life of wholeness, peace, and joy in You, things that You and only You can give. I want to fly like an eagle and feel my soul soar. Help me, Father, to walk freely in You.

In Jesus' name, amen.

Love,

Your princess, who wants true freedom

"He sets people free and saves them.
He does miraculous signs and wonders.
He does them in the heavens and on the earth.
He has saved Daniel from the power of the lions."

DANIEL 6:27, NIRV

My King,

WHO SAVES ME BY GRACE

Lord, I so need Your grace. I fail You every day with careless words I speak and selfish things I do. I'm so glad to have a heavenly Father who covers my steps with His grace. Please forgive me for the times I try to justify my actions or try to fix my mistakes on my own, without You. Help me not to give in to sin, but when I do fail, help me not to give up. Thank You for loving me most when I deserve it least. Remind me that I may come to You, a fountain of grace, again and again, as I try and live my life as Your princess. I know that there's nothing I can do to earn Your grace, it's a gift straight from Your heart to mine. Your grace, which is so evident in my life, is a true gift, and I love You for blessing me with it.

In Jesus' name, amen.

Love,

Your princess, who receives Your grace

*Since we have been made right
in God's sight by faith in his promises,
we can have real peace with him
because of what Jesus Christ our Lord has done for us.*

ROMANS 5:1, TLB

Take My yoke upon you and learn of Me,
for I am gentle and humble in heart,
and you will find rest for your souls.

MATTHEW 11:29

My God,
MY PLACE OF REST

*L*ord, I'm *so* tired—physically, emotionally, and spiritually. Please help me rest in Your arms right now. Help me to gain Your perspective on my life.

Father, I can't keep up the pace that my daily to-do list requires. I know You didn't call me to a crazy, filled-up life that is out of control. So I come to You and confess that I can't do it all, and I don't want to try to anymore.

Please give me wisdom as to when to get up and go…and when to lie down and rest. Show me what is important to You, then fill my heart with a constant desire to live it out. Help me, Lord, not to feel guilty when I sit at Your feet a little while each day or when I obey Your command to take a day of rest each week. Help me break free from the bondage of busyness and enter into a life of peace and divine purpose.

In Jesus' name I pray.

Love,

Your princess, who loves You and longs to rest in You

*O LORD, you have examined my heart
and know everything about me.
You know when I sit down or stand up.
You know my every thought when far away.
You chart the path ahead of me
and tell me where to stop and rest.
Every moment you know where I am.*

PSALM 139:1–3, NLT

My King,
THE KEEPER OF TIME

Lord, help me not to waste my days doing things that don't matter for eternity. I feel as if I allow anything and everything to consume my time. I know that my days are numbered, so I want to be wise when I write something on my calendar. You've given me a limited amount of time to live my life, so keep me mindful of how finite and precious my time on this earth really is. I give You permission to clear my schedule of anything that is keeping me from the divine appointments You have for me, and I submit the rest of my days to You.

In Jesus' name, amen.

Love,

Your princess, who wants to live by Your schedule

My God,
MY CREATOR

*L*ord, it is You who formed my body, crafted my mind, and created my soul. You made me in Your image, and You call me Your own. Therefore I ask You to mold my character so that it displays to the world what You can do with a life surrendered to You. I give You the shattered pieces of my life caused by my sin and my mistakes, and I ask You to put it back together with Your Word, in Your way, and by Your loving Spirit. You are the Master Potter, and I am the clay resting on Your potter's wheel. Please make me a masterpiece—not for my glory, but for Yours.

In Jesus' name, amen.

Love,

Your princess, who is clay in Your hands

O LORD, YOU ARE OUR FATHER;
WE ARE THE CLAY, AND YOU OUR POTTER,
AND WE ALL ARE THE WORK OF YOUR HAND.
ISAIAH 64:8

My King,
YOU ARE MY PROTECTOR

*L*ord, thank You for the privilege of asking You to surround me with Your hedge of protection. Thank You for sending Your angels to stand watch over me. Thank You for Your Spirit living inside of me, and for giving me wisdom and guidance along the way.

Now I humbly ask You to help me rely on Your Spirit and the truth of Your Word as, moment by moment, I travel life's journey. I don't want to fall. I want to walk in Your strength and in obedience to You. I love You, and I choose by faith to trust that You, my Protector and Guide, will keep me safely on Your straight and narrow path.

In Jesus' name I pray.

Love,

Your princess, who hides herself in You

You are my hiding place;

you will protect me from trouble

and surround me with songs of deliverance.

Selah.

PSALM 32:7, NIV

Keep your lives free from the love of money
and be content with what you have,
because God has said,
"Never will I leave you; never will I forsake you."

HEBREWS 13:5, NIV

My King,
MY SOURCE OF CONTENTMENT

*L*ord, You have always given all I've needed and much that I've desired. Yet I confess that I often find myself wanting more. Please show me the root of my discontentment and reveal to me what's not right in my heart. Please teach me to be content no matter where I am and no matter what I have—or don't have. Show me how to let You fill me with Your thirst-quenching peace and Your soul-satisfying joy. Keep me from falling into the worldly trap of wanting what everyone else has instead of being thankful for what You have already so generously given me. Help me not to long for more than what You want me to have. Help me to want *You* more than any other thing around me. And finally, Lord, teach me to be a good steward of the many blessings You have so freely given out of Your love for me.

In Jesus' name, amen.

Love,

Your princess, who longs for contentment in You

My King,

YOU ARE WORDS OF LIFE

Lord, I love You so much. I want to know You better and walk closer with You more than ever before. So why do I struggle to sit and read Your Word? Rather than live my priorities, I seem to place everything else ahead of spending time with You.

God, please grow in me a stronger passion for Your powerful Word. Remind me that every love letter was written just for me and that each one is full of life-giving truth to live by. Don't let me look for wisdom in this world any longer, but instead remind me by Your Holy Spirit that all I need to know about how to live can be found in my Bible.

So I ask You now to help me make time to spend with You regularly in Your precious Word, Your love gift to me. I pray that all You have to say to me will rest securely in my heart and mind as I gain a deeper understanding of who You are and how much You love me.

In Jesus' name I pray.

Love,

Your princess, who wants to know Your Word

The voice of the Lord is powerful;
the voice of the Lord is full of majesty.

PSALM 29:4

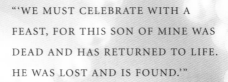

"'WE MUST CELEBRATE WITH A
FEAST, FOR THIS SON OF MINE WAS
DEAD AND HAS RETURNED TO LIFE.
HE WAS LOST AND IS FOUND.'"

LUKE 15:23-24, TLB

My God,
WHO FOUND ME

*L*ord, thank You for calling me and leading me to You when I was walking aimlessly through life. Let me *never* forget where I came from and where I am now because You loved me enough to pursue me and bring me home to You.

I know that now You want to use me to lead others that are lost and lonely to You, so they too can know of Your love for them. I know that You also call me to help the hurting and minister to the poor. But sometimes, Lord, I feel empty, too empty to fill others up, and confused about what is needed to offer godly direction.

So, when I'm with someone who doesn't know You, help me not to depend on myself, but to depend on You for strength and direction. I know—but I forget—that You will enable me to do whatever You call me to do. And anoint my lips with Your words of life that will guide them to Your welcoming and loving arms.

In Jesus' name, amen.

Love,

Your princess, who needs Your divine direction

My King,

YOU ARE MY ANSWER TO EVERYTHING

Lord, You are my answer to everything. There is no one like You. Whatever I need, You supply. Whenever I'm confused, Your Word clears my mind and sets my mind at rest.

Lord, I want You to use me to do great things for Your kingdom. I don't want past disappointments to keep me from responding with anything but passion and purpose to the call You have on my life. So today I am asking You for the greatest desire of my heart: Please make my life matter for eternity. Guide my steps toward that great goal and continue to bless me with all I need to serve You. Help me to never give up or give in to anything but You. You truly are all that I need or want!

In Jesus' name, amen.

Love,

Your princess, who wants whatever You have for me

Now glory be to God
who by his mighty power at work within us
is able to do far more
than we would ever dare to ask or even dream of—
infinitely beyond our highest prayers,
desires, thoughts, or hopes.

EPHESIANS 3:20, TLB

For it is by grace you have been saved,
through faith—
and this not from yourselves,
it is the gift of God.

EPHESIANS 2:8, NIV

My King,

WHO SENT YOUR SON, MY SAVIOR

*J*esus, I can be overwhelmed by my sinful nature, and when that happens I'm tempted to try to hide from You. I find myself weighed down by shame and afraid to confess my true feelings.

Please help me, Lord, to be honest and genuine with You when I need to repent of my sin. Convict me when I am trying to hide secret sin from You. Give me the courage to go to You and let You cleanse me, heal me, and give me a new start. Help me accept the wondrous truth that You died for me so that I could be free!

I need You, Lord God. I can't live my life without Your love, Your power, and Your forgiveness. Help me not only to fully receive Your forgiveness, but to be able to forgive myself when I fail. I am ready to start fresh and new and thank You for being a God of unlimited second chances!

In Your name I pray.

Love,

Your princess, who needs Your forgiveness

My God,

YOU MAKE ME NEW

*L*ord, Your Word teaches that I am a new creation, that I am not the same person I was before I met You, and that the old me is gone. I want to believe that, but I need Your help.

Please show me how to live as the new person that You have made me. Renew my mind, my spirit, and my image of myself. I want to be the princess You have created me to be. Show me the people and things I need to walk away from so that I can walk more closely with You. Wash me as white as snow. Put in me a clean heart, a heart that longs for Your love and approval.

Trusting in Your faithfulness, I thank You for what You are doing in me, and I thank You for what I will become. Thank You for giving Your life to pay the price for my sin. Thank You that the Holy Spirit's power that raised You from the dead is in me, a new creation.

In Jesus' name I pray.

Love,

Your princess, who is a new creation

Let us go right in, to God himself,
with true hearts fully trusting him to receive us,
because we have been sprinkled with Christ's blood
to make us clean,
and because our bodies have been washed with pure water.

HEBREWS 10:22, TLB

My King,

YOU KNOW WHAT'S BEST FOR ME

*L*ord, sometimes I am so discouraged by the way situations work out—by the way my plans for my life fail. My hopes and dreams dissolve into disappointment, and I find myself feeling hopeless. When I'm at that place, help me trust You more. Help me know that You are working on my behalf even when I don't see things happening the way I want them to. Give me the strength to keep doing the right thing—to keep obeying and trusting You—even when everything seems to be going wrong. I ask You to renew my hope and open my eyes to the spiritual significance of life's disappointments, challenges, and frustrations. I am choosing to believe that You, my Father, know what is best for me, and that You're in control of the tiniest details in my life.

In Jesus' name I pray.

Love,

Your princess, who wants Your will for my life

And we know that God causes all things
to work together for good
to those who love God,
to those who are called according to His purpose.

ROMANS 8:28, NASB

*God has actually given us his Spirit
to tell us about the wonderful free gifts
of grace and blessing that God has given us.*

1 CORINTHIANS 2:12, TLB

My King,

YOU HAVE SET ME APART

Lord, I know that You call me to be different from the world, to live a life that reflects that I am Yours. Everything in me wants to follow You and live as Your princess. But sometimes I feel overwhelmed by Your call. I fight against my desires to do things the easy way, the world's way, instead of the right way, Your way. I feel as if I can never be the person I want to be for You. In those moments remind me by Your spirit who I am and how powerful You are. I know that apart from You I can do nothing of value. So please, God, help me to cling to the power of Your supernatural strength and to be in this world without becoming part of it.

In Jesus' name, amen.

Love,

Your princess, Your chosen one

*My soul yearns, even faints,
for the courts of the LORD;
my heart and my flesh cry out
for the living God.*

PSALM 84:2, NIV

My God,
PLEASE WIPE AWAY MY TEARS

Lord, I want to have a more open relationship with You. Like King David, I want to be a woman after Your heart. Like him, I want to be able to freely share my heart, my sin, my pain, and my hurts.

I have lived so long trying to hide my private pain and handle everything myself.

I fear that if I cry out to You, the tears locked inside me will never stop flowing. Because I have never felt completely safe with anyone before, it's hard for me to believe that You, the God of all the universe, would come to me personally, wipe away my tears, and heal my heart.

Release me and help me to cry out to You so I can be free. Hold me with Your mighty, tender hands and love me back to a life of wholeness again.

In Jesus' name, amen.

Love,

Your princess, who longs to be held and healed by You

My King,
CAPTAIN OF MY LIFE

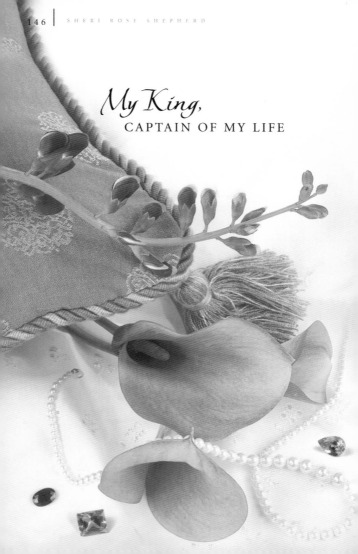

*L*ord, it seems that life is one big storm after another. And as the storms rage, I find myself fearing that I will be washed away if I don't take control of my own life. Yet I know that You want me to let go of my life instead of thinking and acting as if I'm in control. Please give me the courage to rest in You when life's overwhelming storms rage. Teach me to trust You through the bad-weather days—and not to forget You when the sailing is smooth. I no longer want to try to control either the circumstances of my life or the people around me. I'm ready once again to have You guide me through my days. And, as I pray, I ask You to calm the biggest storm of all—the one of nervousness and anxiety that too often rages inside of me. Thank You that You are the captain of my life and the Living Water that calms my soul.

In Jesus' name I pray.

Love,

Your princess, who is handing over control of my life

THIS IS WHAT THE LORD SAYS:
"STAND AT THE CROSSROADS AND LOOK;
ASK FOR THE ANCIENT PATHS,
ASK WHERE THE GOOD WAY IS, AND WALK IN IT,
AND YOU WILL FIND REST FOR YOUR SOULS."

JEREMIAH 6:16, NIV

My King,
GIVER OF LIFE

Lord, sometimes I can be so selfish. I get too consumed with myself—*my* wants, *my* needs, and *my* desires. Please help me be aware of the times when I'm self-absorbed. Lord, stop me before I sink into that pit!

I want to be more like You, Lord. You have given me life itself. You have sacrificed Your life so I could live in victory. I need to know the true joy of giving to others unconditionally just as You have given to me. So I'm asking You to make my heart compassionate. Keep my mind fixed on the needs of others. Forgive me for not extending Your acts of lovingkindness to people I know who are looking to be loved. Break me of the sinful tendency to take all I can get, and instead change my attitude to give all I can give and to glorify who You are inside of me.

In Jesus' name, amen.

Love,

Your princess, who wants to give as You have given

Therefore, as God's chosen people,

holy and dearly loved,

clothe yourselves with compassion, kindness,

humility, gentleness and patience.

COLOSSIANS 3:12, NIV

"For even I, the Son of Man,
came here not to be served
but to serve others,
and to give my life as a ransom for many."

MARK 10:45, NLT

My God,
WHO'S PAID THE PRICE

Jesus, it's so amazing to me that You paid the price for my sin with Your life. You loved me before I ever even thought about You. Yet too often I walk away from Your love. Forgive me for taking Your presence and Your love for granted. And forgive me for not counting the cost of my poor choices before I make them. Help me to value my life as the precious gift that it is. I don't want to sell out to a world that's trying to steal my integrity, corrupt my character, and weaken my love for You. Please protect me, guide me, and help me to spend my time here wisely. Show me how You want me to invest the talents and gifts that You have given me for Your eternal purposes. And let me never forget the true and lasting value of what You did for me on the cross, the price You paid, just for me.

In Your name I pray.

Love,

Your princess, who is grateful for everlasting life

My God,

SET ME FREE TO BE ME

*L*ord, I so need and want to be real in my relationship with You. But for too long I have pretended to be someone I am not. Now it's hard for me to know what I truly think or feel, or who I really am. Please help me see more clearly who You have created me to be. Deliver me from the tendency to try to be some perfect person in order to win people's approval. I know that's bondage, and I ask that You set me free! Help me live for Your approval alone. Set me free from *myself* and help me express what I really feel and care about when I pray. I don't want a superficial relationship with You. I want to be real with You—no more pretending!

In Jesus' name, amen.

Love,

Your princess, who wants a genuine relationship with You

My dwelling place will be with them;
I will be their God,
and they will be my people.

EZEKIEL 37:27, NIV

AND SO BLESSING AND CURSING
COME POURING OUT OF THE SAME MOUTH.
SURELY, MY BROTHERS AND SISTERS,
THIS IS NOT RIGHT!

JAMES 3:10, NLT

My King,
ANOINT MY LIPS

Lord, I want to speak Your words of life and love to the world. But daily I'm tempted to talk about others in a way that tears them down rather than builds them up. I need You to take control of my tongue. Forgive me for speaking words that hurt when I have the power to say something that would heal. Forgive me for not first coming to You to anoint my conversations. Please convict me when I carelessly say things that don't reflect who You are in me. Remind me that I am royalty and that I need to speak like the princess You've called me to be, and speak words of life.

In Jesus' name, amen.

Love,

Your princess, who wants to speak Your words

My God,

YOU REMOVE MY GUILT

*L*ord, I can't help but look back on my life with guilt and regret. I think about the things that I shouldn't have done or said and all the things that I could have done. I reflect on the times that I brought shame to You and myself, and pain to others. I know that Your Word says You have washed me white as snow and that You want me to let go of my guilt over what has gone wrong. But I can't do it without Your help. Please renew my mind with Your Word and help me to accept that You died for *all* my mistakes and sins. Help me to believe that I can become a new person with a new start in You. I'm ready to be free from the guilt of my past, and move on to a life of victory and purpose in You.

In Jesus' name I pray.

Love,

Your princess, who accepts Your cleansing

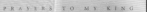

You are cleansed and pruned already,
because of the word which I have given you.

JOHN 15:3

"Come to me and I will give you rest—
all of you who work so hard beneath a heavy yoke.
Wear my yoke—for it fits perfectly—
and let me teach you; for I am gentle and humble,
and you shall find rest for your souls;
for I give you only light burdens."

MATTHEW 11:28–30, TLB

My King,
HELP DEFINE MY BOUNDARIES

*L*ord, my schedule is so out of control! I'm caught up daily in excessive busyness as too many responsibilities, activities, and people pull me in different directions. I know that You don't want me to exhaust myself by trying to do all that I've been doing. And I know that You don't want me to continue abusing my body, Your temple, with the unrealistic demands I've been putting on myself.

So please show me how to say no, even when Satan threatens me with false guilt. Please give me the wisdom I need to prioritize my schedule so that I'm living the way You want me to. Teach me to walk through life being led and controlled by Your Spirit alone.

In Jesus' name I pray.

Love,

Your princess, who needs Your help setting boundaries

My King,

ORDER MY STEPS
THAT I MIGHT DO GOOD

*L*ord, I want You to use me today, so please order my steps. Open my eyes so that I will see the needs of those around me. Don't let me miss out on the good works You have planned for me to do today. Let me extend an act of kindness or offer a word of encouragement to someone who needs to see Your hand in their life.

Thank You for choosing me to be one of Your representatives in this dark world. Never let me forget that I'm here on this earth to be a channel of Your love, peace, and power in a world that is lost without You.

In Jesus' name, amen.

Love,

Your princess, who longs to walk in Your ways

For we are God's masterpiece.
He has created us anew in Christ Jesus,
so that we can do the good things
he planned for us long ago.

EPHESIANS 2:10, NLT

My King,
YOUR SPIRIT DWELLS IN ME

*L*ord, keep me mindful that my body is Your dwelling place, the temple of Your Holy Spirit. Forgive me for the times that I make Your temple my trash can. Too often I abuse myself with the things I read and watch; too often I defile Your temple with what or how much I eat.

Lord, You alone deserve honor and worship, so teach me to honor You with my body, my mind, and my spirit. You have sacrificed Your only Son for me, and You have blessed me beyond measure with Your protection, Your provision, and Your very presence with me. The least I can do is give up the unhealthy worldly pleasures that weaken, if not destroy, my body. Give me the self-discipline and wisdom to take care of what is Yours—my body. Help me to be holy and pure in Your sight.

In Jesus' name I pray.

Love,

Your princess, a temple of Your Holy Spirit

Splendor and majesty are before him;
strength and joy in his dwelling place.

1 CHRONICLES 16:27, NIV

And you must love the LORD your God
with all your heart,
all your soul,
and all your strength.

DEUTERONOMY 6:5, NLT

My King,

I NEED YOUR LOVE

*L*ord, I don't want to play any more games in an attempt to get love from a man. I'm tired of trying hard to get attention and approval from men instead of from You. Deliver me into Your arms of true love, the only place I'll find attention that lasts and approval that matters.

Show me the men I have allowed in my life who are distracting me from You. Give me the wisdom to know who they are and the strength to end those relationships now. I am ready to put You first and fall in love with You all over again—I'm ready to love You with all that I am. And in Your perfect timing, whenever that is, please reveal to me the man who is sent from You alone, for a relationship that will be rooted in You and will bring You honor and glory when we are together.

In Jesus' name, amen.

Love,

Your princess, who wants to love You most of all

Now you can have sincere love for each
other as brothers and sisters because
you were cleansed from your sins
when you accepted the truth of the Good News.
So see to it that you really do love each other
intensely with all your hearts.

1 PETER 1:22, NLT

My King,
HELP ME ACCEPT OTHERS

Lord, I need You to help me accept other people's faults and weaknesses with the same grace, forgiveness, and tolerance that You extend to me. Who am I, that I should place myself above anyone else? I know that's what I'm doing when I look down on others who are struggling just as I struggle, only in other ways. Please let me never forget that I am a sinner, saved only because of Your amazing grace. Give me a heart to love the unlovable and an extra dose of compassion to care for those who are hurting or hard to deal with. Forgive me for rejecting people because they are not perfect. I know that only You are perfect and that we all need Your love and grace to survive each day of life on this earth.

In Jesus' name, amen.

Love,

Your princess, who is grateful for Your acceptance

My King,

HELP ME SEE WHO I TRULY AM

$\mathcal{L}$ord, too often when I look in the mirror, I don't like the reflection I see. Deep in my heart, I see someone who is hardly good enough to do anything great for You. I try to remind myself how special I am in Your eyes and that Your strength is made perfect in my weakness.

But, still, my eyes are often blinded by my own insecurities and imperfections. I am haunted by hurtful things people have said to me. I don't want to buy the lies that run through my head saying I'm worthless, so I'm crying out to You now with all my heart. You know the reasons why I don't like myself. I don't want those thoughts to keep me from walking in Your confidence. I ask You, Lord, to give me a new and clearer reflection of who I *truly* am. I want to let Your loving face be my mirror.

In Jesus' name I pray.

Love,

Your princess, whose image needs Your divine touch

"MY GRACE IS SUFFICIENT FOR YOU,
FOR MY POWER IS MADE PERFECT IN WEAKNESS."
THEREFORE I WILL BOAST ALL THE MORE GLADLY
ABOUT MY WEAKNESSES,
SO THAT CHRIST'S POWER MAY REST ON ME.

2 CORINTHIANS 12:9, NIV

My God,
YOU ARE TRUE LOVE

*L*ord, sometimes I am so confused about love. I have had people tell me that they love me—and then hurt me terribly. Is love supposed to hurt? Is it more than an emotion or an act of kindness? I see marriages all around me that reflect everything but love. Is it more than a vow of commitment?

Heal my heart from those who have made love painful so that I may more fully receive and share Your love. Give me wisdom to know the difference between real love and the world's counterfeit version. Teach me Your definition of love and by Your Spirit, show me how to extend that love to others. Through Your Word and prayer I'm ready to gain a new and better understanding of Your amazing, sacrificial love—a love that builds others up and points people to You. A love everlasting.

In Jesus' name, amen.

Love,

Your princess, who wants to know true love

May you be able to feel and understand,
as all God's children should,
how long, how wide, how deep,
and how high his love really is;
and to experience this love for yourselves....

EPHESIANS 3:18, TLB

For you have a new life.
It was not passed on to you from your parents,
for the life they gave you will fade away.
This new one will last forever,
for it comes from Christ,
God's ever-living Message to men.

1 PETER 1:23, TLB

My King,
I WANT TO LIVE WITH YOU FOREVER

*L*ord, Your Word says that my eyes have not seen, nor my ears heard, nor my mind imagined the place that You have prepared for me in heaven. Sometimes I am filled with excitement about seeing You face-to-face, but at other times I don't give any thought to who You are or what You are building for me. Forgive me for my thoughtlessness. Please prompt me to meditate more on my home in heaven and less on the material things I think I need here and now. I want to live my life in constant anticipation of that great day when I am fully in Your presence, where there will be no more tears, no more pain, but a place where there will be neverending peace and praise to You, our King!

In Jesus' name, amen.

Love,

Your princess, who can't wait to be home with You

My King,

WHO DELIGHTS IN ME

Lord, Your Word says that no one delights in me more than You do! I am Your daughter, chosen and adopted by You, who wants to make You proud. I want You to look at me and say, "That's My girl, doing My will!"

I love You, Lord, and I am humbled and grateful that You delight in me. Help me keep my mind fixed on You. Remind me moment by moment that I am a daughter of the King of kings. Don't let me get distracted from Your purposes for me and teach me how to let You guide my steps. Continue to lead me in every stage of my life. As I seek You first, may I know the blessings of Your care and especially the blessings of Your loving presence with me.

In Jesus' name, amen.

Love,

Your princess, who delights in You

The LORD delights in those who fear him,
who put their hope in his unfailing love.

PSALM 147:11, NIV

SING FOR JOY, O HEAVENS;

SHOUT, O EARTH.

BREAK FORTH WITH SONG,

O MOUNTAINS, FOR THE LORD

HAS COMFORTED HIS PEOPLE,

AND WILL HAVE COMPASSION

UPON THEM IN THEIR SORROW.

ISAIAH 49:13, TLB

My God,
YOU ARE MY SHELTER

Lord, thank You for being my safe place in this lost and threatening world. Only in You can I find real shelter and security. I am so grateful that You are never too busy to provide me with a safe place of peace and hope, of respite and rest. You are always available for Your daughter.

How blessed I am that the God of all the earth is my Refuge and my Strength, my Comfort and my Father. I love You more than words can express, and I am so amazed at how You walk with me through my life, always sheltering me with Your mighty hand. Thank You that I am never alone in any circumstance. You are here with me wherever I go. Thank You that You are a constant source of safety, comfort, and refuge. I love You, Lord.

In Jesus' name, amen.

Love,

Your princess, who finds shelter in You

My King,

YOU ALONE ARE EXCELLENT!

*L*ord, don't let me settle for a life of mediocrity. I want to live a life of excellence, a life that reflects *Your* excellence.

Give me the strength to do the right thing, no matter how hard, in a world that continually tempts everyone to compromise. Grant me the ability to live in a way that points people to You and that influences for Your kingdom all who are watching. Let me be one who helps others realize not only their full potential, but the freedom they can have in a relationship with You.

I know that You can do anything. So please, use me to model a higher and holy standard—a standard of godly excellence—for the next generation to live by. Let my life leave a legacy for You!

In Jesus' name, amen.

Love,

Your princess, who wants to reflect Your excellence

*A*nd I want you to stress these things,
so that those who have trusted in God
may be careful to devote themselves
to doing what is good.
These things are excellent
and profitable for everyone.

TITUS 3:8, NIV

All our greatness is like a flower
that droops and falls;
but the Word of the Lord will last forever.
And his message is the Good News
that was preached to you.

1 PETER 1:24–25, TLB

My King,

HELP ME CHOOSE LIFE IN YOU

*L*ord, You have given me the choice between life and death, between knowing Your blessing and turning from it.

God, I want the abundant life You offer; I want to receive and acknowledge Your blessings in my life. And I know that the only way to experience that kind of life is to obey Your Word. But I know myself, and I know that obedience doesn't come easily or naturally for me. My sin nature weakens my will and makes it too easy for me to do the things I don't want to do, and not do the things I *want* to do! And I don't want to blow it!

Lord, I know I can't do it alone. I need the accountability of a sister in Christ, but I don't know whom to turn to. Please send someone, handpicked by You, to help guard my way and to grow with me— someone to share in the journey before me. And one day when my foundation in You is firm, let me do the same. All for Your glory and Your kingdom. Today I choose life!

In Jesus' name, amen.

Love,

Your princess, who chooses life in You

My King,

MAY I LEAVE A LEGACY OF YOU

Lord, I want to leave a legacy for You. I want to say, "As for me and my house, we will serve the Lord." Let those I love look at my life as a model of You.

Grant me wisdom so that I will make godly choices in a world that says anything is acceptable. Give me hope in You that I can pass on to my loved ones. Let me experience the contagious joy that comes with living for You and furthering Your kingdom. Bless my children and their future, as You promise in Your Word You'll do if I love You and keep Your commands.

Lord, I want to be remembered as a woman whose character paved the way for faith and success for the next generation. May I leave a permanent mark of Your love on the hearts of all who know me.

In Jesus' name, amen.

Love,

Your princess, who wants to leave a legacy of

Your love

"The Lord your God is the faithful God
who for a thousand generations
keeps his promises and constantly loves
those who love him and who obey his commands."

DEUTERONOMY 7:9, TLB

My King,

YOU ARE THE BEGINNING AND THE END

Lord, You are the Alpha and the Omega, the Beginning and the End. Help me remember that my first breath began with You and that my last will lead me to my final resting place with You. I know this truth well, but sometimes, Lord, I fear how my life will end and what the other side of eternity will be like.

Give me freedom from that fear of death and grant me peace of mind, the peace of mind that comes only from knowing heaven is my real home and Jesus is my Savior. Help me rest in this truth. Remind me that I am Your bride and that great rewards await me when I am finally home.

Thank You that You number my days and that my life will not end when I die; rather, it's just the beginning of truly knowing You and seeing You face-to-face. Thank You that You are preparing a place for me even now, while I'm praying. Thank You for the privilege of being put here on earth to reign as Your princess. How blessed I am to spend eternity with You!

In Jesus' name, amen.

Love,

Your princess, who began and will end with You

"It is finished!
I am the A and the Z—
the Beginning and the End.
I will give to the thirsty
the springs of the Water of Life—as a gift!
Everyone who conquers
will inherit all these blessings, and I will be his God...."

REVELATION 21:6–7, TLB

I'd love to
HEAR FROM YOU!

*T*o write Sheri Rose personally,
or for booking information and
to see her line of *His Princess*™ jewelry
(a beautiful reminder that
we are Daughters of the King),
visit her website at
www.HisPrincess.com
or call 602-407-8789.